Hurricanes

by Matt Doeden

Lerner Publications Company • Minneapolis

Photo Acknowledgments

The images in this book are used with the permission of: © Christopher Harris/SuperStock, p. 4; NASA Johnson Space Center-Earth Sciences and Image Analysis, p. 6; © Win McNamee/Getty Images, p. 7; © Klaus Hackenberg/zefa/CORBIS, p. 8; © Roger Ressmeyer/CORBIS, p. 9; © CORBIS, p. 10; © Erik Von Weber/Stone/Getty Images, p. 11; © Jim Reed/CORBIS, pp. 12, 24; © DANIEL LECLAIR/Reuters/CORBIS, p. 14; © DANIEL AGUILAR/Reuters/CORBIS, pp. 15, 27; © Steve Liss/Time & Life Pictures/Getty Images, p. 16; Courtesy of the National Oceanic and Atmospheric Administration Central Library Photo Collection, p. 18; © Vincent Laforet/Pool/Reuters/CORBIS, p. 19; © FRANCOIS GOEMANS/AFP/Getty Images, p. 20; © China Photos/Getty Images, p. 21; AP Photo/Andy Newman, p. 22; © Joe Raedle/Getty Images, p. 25; © Barbara Davidson/Dallas Morning News/CORBIS, p. 26.

Front Cover: © Mike Theiss/CORBIS.

Lerner Publications Company
A division of Lerner Publishing Group, Inc.
241 First Avenue North
Minneapolis, MN 55401 U.S.A.

Website address: www.lernerbooks.com

Words in **bold type** are explained in a glossary on page 31.

Library of Congress Cataloging-in-Publication Data

Doeden, Matt.
    Hurricanes / by Matt Doeden.
        p.   cm. – (Pull ahead books. Forces of nature)
    Includes index.
    ISBN-13: 978-0-8225-7906-9 (lib. bdg. : alk. paper)
    1. Hurricanes—Juvenile literature. I. Title.
    QC944.2.D64 2008
    551.55'2–dc22   2007022579

Manufactured in the United States of America
1 2 3 4 5 6 – JR – 13 12 11 10 09 08

Table of Contents

What Is a Hurricane?

Strong winds blow. Tall waves crash against the coast. What kind of storm is this?

This huge storm is a **hurricane.**
Hurricanes start over the ocean.
Clouds form in warm, wet air above
the ocean.

A hurricane seen from space

The clouds grow larger. They begin to turn like a huge wheel. The clouds become a **tropical storm.**

Heavy rains fall from the storm clouds.
Lightning and thunder crash in the sky.

Around the outside of the storm, the winds become stronger and stronger.

Strong winds from a hurricane make big waves in the ocean.

But in the storm's center, a calm area called the **eye** forms.

The storm becomes a hurricane. Winds
push the hurricane toward the coast.

The Hurricane Reaches Land

A hurricane has very strong winds. The winds push water from the ocean toward land. A **storm surge** forms. High waves smash onto the coast. The hurricane's winds blow rain sideways. Tornadoes may form too. Tornadoes are dangerous, spinning windstorms.

A hurricane's storm surge and rain can cause terrible **floods**.

The storm's winds can flatten buildings. Cars may roll over. Beaches, trees, and towns may be destroyed.

When and Where Hurricanes Happen

Hurricanes can form anytime. But most hurricanes happen between June and November. Many hurricanes begin in the Atlantic Ocean. Some of these hurricanes strike the east coast of North America. Others enter the Gulf of Mexico.

A terrible hurricane hit the Gulf Coast in 2005. It was called Hurricane Katrina.

Hurricane Katrina seen from space

Hurricane Katrina almost destroyed
the city of New Orleans, Louisiana.
Do hurricanes happen in other parts
of the world?

Huge storms that are like hurricanes start in the Indian Ocean. These storms are called **cyclones**. They may strike India or Africa.

Cyclone Flavio destroyed this village in Africa.

Typhoon Haitang in China

Huge storms like hurricanes also start in the Pacific Ocean. They are called **typhoons.** They often hit China, Japan, and other countries in western Asia.

Staying Safe

Scientists watch tropical storms and hurricanes. They give each storm a name. They figure out where it will go. Then they warn people who live in the storm's path. Some people **evacuate.** They leave their homes to get to safety.

Other people stay behind. They nail boards over windows so strong winds will not break them.

They tie down things that could blow away. Then they go inside and wait for the storm to pass.

After the storm, people step outside to see the damage. Sometimes whole towns have to be rebuilt.

Hurricanes are strong, deadly storms. They show us the power of nature.

MORE ABOUT HURRICANES

Scientists use the Saffir-Simpson Hurricane Scale to compare the strength of different hurricanes. The scale has five groups called categories. Category 1 hurricanes have the slowest winds and cause the least damage. Category 5 hurricanes have the fastest winds and cause the most damage.

Category	Wind Speed (miles per hour)	Amount of Damage
1	74 to 95	Leaves blow off bushes and trees.
2	96 to 110	Some roofs, doors, and windows are damaged. Some trees are blown down.
3	111 to 130	Some small buildings are damaged. Some large trees are blown down.
4	131 to 155	Roofs are blown off of houses. Doors and windows break.
5	more than 155	Wind completely destroys some buildings. All bushes and trees are blown down.

HURRICANE FACTS

- Hurricanes are huge storms. Most hurricanes are about 300 miles across. That's as wide as the state of Pennsylvania.

- A hurricane can last for more than two weeks.

- The first hurricane each year gets a name starting with the letter A. The second storm's name starts with a B, and so on. The names take turns between men's names and women's names.

- Around a hurricane's eye is a wall of clouds called the eye wall. The storm's strongest winds are in the eye wall.

- The deadliest hurricane in the United States hit Galveston, Texas, in 1900. A storm surge 20 feet high rushed through the city. More than 8,000 people were killed.

Further Reading

Books

Berger, Melvin, and Gilda Berger. *Hurricanes Have Eyes But Can't See: And Other Amazing Facts about Wild Weather.* New York: Scholastic, 2004.

Demarest, Chris L. *Hurricane Hunters!: Riders on the Storm.* New York: Margaret K. McElderry Books, 2006.

Jango-Cohen, Judith. *Why Does It Rain?* Minneapolis: Millbrook Press, 2006.

Websites

Aim a Hurricane
http://www.nhc.noaa.gov/HAW2/english/kids/movncane.htm
Use this online simulator to see how winds move a hurricane.

Hurricane: Storm Science
http://www.miamisci.org/hurricane
This website shows how to make your own tools to study the weather, and lets you see inside a hurricane.

Hurricanes
http://www.fema.gov/kids/hurr.htm
This website has information about how hurricanes start, hurricane names, and what to do if a hurricane is coming to your area.

Glossary

cyclones: huge storms that are like hurricanes. Cyclones start in the Indian Ocean.

evacuate: to go to a safer place

eye: the center of a hurricane

floods: large amounts of water covering places that are usually dry

hurricane: a huge storm that starts over warm ocean water. The speed of a hurricane's winds is at least 74 miles per hour.

storm surge: high water that a hurricane's winds push from the ocean onto the shore

tropical storm: a big storm with winds blowing 39 to 73 miles per hour

typhoons: huge storms that are like hurricanes. Typhoons start in the Pacific Ocean.

Index